PARAMAHANSA YOGANANDA
(1893–1952)

METAPHYSICAL MEDITATIONS

UNIVERSAL PRAYERS, AFFIRMATIONS, AND VISUALIZATIONS

BY

PARAMAHANSA
YOGANANDA

Self-Realization Fellowship

FOUNDED 1920

Paramahansa Yogananda

Authorized by the International Publications Council of
SELF-REALIZATION FELLOWSHIP
3880 San Rafael Avenue • Los Angeles, CA 90065-3298

The Self-Realization Fellowship name and emblem (shown above) appears on all SRF books, recordings, and other publications, assuring the
reader that a work originates with the society established by Paramahansa
Yogananda and faithfully conveys his teachings.

ISBN 0-87612-047-8
Printed in the United States of America
12723-54321

ABOUT THIS BOOK

Throughout his early years in America, in the public lectures and classes he gave during extensive speaking tours—and in later years at the Self-Realization Fellowship temples he founded—Paramahansa Yogananda would often lead his audiences in an affirmation, visualization, or prayerful invocation. Reflecting the myriad ways in which the Infinite Spirit may be addressed and perceived, these metaphysical methods had a wide appeal. After 1925, when Sri Yogananda established in Los Angeles an international headquarters for his society and began publishing the magazine *East-West* (which he renamed *Self-Realization* in 1948), many such meditations were printed in the magazine; and in 1932 a collection of nearly 200 of them was published by Self-Realization Fellowship in *Metaphysical Meditations*. The book has been in continuous publication ever since, with expanded editions appearing in 1952 and 1964. Offering a wellspring of hope and inspiration, it has found a growing audience of appreciative readers among those of all faiths.

SELF-REALIZATION FELLOWSHIP

Prayer for a United World
By Paramahansa Yogananda

MAY THE HEADS of all countries and races be guided to understand that men of all nations are physically and spiritually one: physically one, because we are the descendants of common parents—the symbolic Adam and Eve; and spiritually one, because we are the immortal children of our Father, bound by eternal links of brotherhood.

Let us pray in our hearts for a League of Souls and a United World. Though we may seem divided by race, creed, color, class, and political prejudices, still, as children of the one God we are able in our souls to feel brotherhood and world unity. May we work for the creation of a United World in which every nation will be a useful part, guided by God through man's enlightened conscience.

In our hearts we can all learn to be free from hate and selfishness. Let us pray for harmony among the nations, that they march hand in hand through the gate of a fair new civilization.

FOREWORD

MEDITATION IS THE science of God-realization. It is
the most practical science in the world. Most people would want to meditate if they understood its
value and experienced its beneficial effects. The ultimate object of meditation is to attain conscious
awareness of God, and of the soul's eternal oneness
with Him. What achievement could be more pur-
poseful and useful than to harness limited human
faculties to the omnipresence and omnipotence of
the Creator? God-realization bestows on the medi-
tator the blessings of the Lord's peace, love, joy,
power, and wisdom.

Meditation utilizes concentration in its highest
form. Concentration consists in freeing the attention from distractions and in focusing it on any
thought in which one may be interested. Meditation
is that special form of concentration in which the attention has been liberated from restlessness and is
focused on God. Meditation, therefore, is concentration used to know God.*

* Complete instruction in the theory and practice of the scientific

In response to the love of exalted devotees, God has manifested Himself in various cosmic forms. He also manifests Himself in truth, in divine qualities, in the creative power and beauty in nature, in the lives of great saints and avatars (divine incarnations), and in the soul of every human being. Thus meditation on any of these concepts brings a deep realization of the omnipresent Absolute, of Him who is ever-existing, ever-conscious, ever-new Bliss. And because meditation gives direct perception of God, it raises the practice of religion above the differences of dogma.

In this book are meditations of three types: prayers or loving demands addressed to God, affirmations about God or truth, and spiritual guidance and inspiration to be directed to one's own consciousness. Select a meditation that meets your present need. To help focus your mind on that spiritual thought, practice the following meditation instructions: Sit on a straight chair, or in a cross-legged po-

---

methods of meditation taught by Paramahansa Yogananda is given in the *Self-Realization Fellowship Lessons.*

sition on a firm surface. Keep the spine straight and the chin parallel to the floor. With eyes closed, gently focus your gaze and concentrate your attention at the point between the eyebrows. This is the seat of concentration, and of the spiritual eye, or divine perception, in man. With the attention fixed at this center of calmness and concentration, practice the meditation you have chosen. Audibly or mentally repeat the words slowly, concentrating on them intently until you become absorbed in the inner meaning. Meditate until you feel that the concept on which you are meditating has become a part of your own consciousness.

The first proof of God's presence is an ineffable peace. This evolves into joy humanly inconceivable. Once you have touched the Source of truth and life, all nature will respond to you. Finding God within, you will find Him without, in all people and all conditions.

Contents

If You Want His Answer

By Paramahansa Yogananda

Whether He replies or not,
Keep calling Him—
Ever calling in the chamber
Of continuous prayer.

Whether He comes or not,
Believe He is ever approaching
Nearer to you
With each command of your heart's love.

Whether He answers or not,
Keep entreating Him.
Even if He makes no reply
In the way you expect,
Ever know that in some subtle way
He will respond.

In the darkness of your deepest prayers,
Know that with you He is playing
Hide-and-seek.

And in the midst of the dance of life,
disease, and death,
If you keep calling Him,
Undepressed by His seeming silence,
You will receive His answer.

DEVOTION AND WORSHIP

To Begin a Meditation

LOCK THE EYELID-DOORS and shut out the wild dance of tempting scenes. Drop your mind into the bottomless well of your heart. Hold the mind on your heart that is bubbling with life-giving blood. Keep your attention tied to the heart, until you feel its rhythmic beat. With every heartbeat feel the pulse of almighty Life. Picture the same all-pervading Life knocking at the heart-door of millions of human beings and of billions of other creatures. The heart-throb constantly, meekly announces the presence of Infinite Power behind the doors of your awareness. The gentle beat of all-pervading Life says to you silently, "Do not receive only a little flow of My life, but expand the opening of thy feeling-powers. Let Me flood thy blood, body, mind, feelings, and soul with My throbs of universal life."

To Awaken Mental Freedom

SIT STILL WITH a straight spine. Cover up your fidgety eyeballs with the sheets of your eyelids. Hold them still. Then loosen your mind from the consciousness of body-weight. Relax the nerve-strings that are attached to the heavy muscles and bones of your body. Forget the consciousness of carrying a heavy bundle of bones tied in the thick cloth of flesh. Rest. Free your mind from the consciousness of a beast of burden. Do not think of your body-load, but feel your soul untied from the constant material quality of heaviness. Mentally race in your fancy's airplane above, beneath, left, right, in infinity, or wherever you want to go. Feel and meditate on this, your mental freedom from your body. Dream, dwell, and feel this body-aboveness when sitting still; the consciousness of freedom will constantly increase.

Universal Prayer

MAY THY LOVE shine forever on the sanctuary of my devotion, and may I be able to awaken Thy love in all hearts.

O Father, receive Thou the fervor of my soul, the devotion of incarnations, the love of ages that I have kept locked in the vault of my heart.

Divine Father, in my temple of silence I have made a garden for Thee, decorated with the blossoms of my devotion.

With aspiring heart, with zealous mind, with flaming soul, I lay at Thy feet of omnipresence all the flowers of my devotion.

O Spirit, I worship Thee as beauty and intelligence in the temple of Nature. I worship Thee as power in the temple of activity, and as peace in the temple of silence.

I Will Wait for Thee

IN THE CENTER of my heart I have a mystic throne for Thee. The candles of my joys are dimly lighted in the hope of Thy coming. They will burn brighter when Thou appearest. Whether Thou comest or not, I will wait for Thee until my tears melt away all material grossness.

To please Thee my love-perfumed tears will wash Thy feet of silence. The altar of my soul will be kept empty until Thou comest.

I will talk not; I will ask naught of Thee. I will realize that Thou knowest the pangs of my heart while I wait for Thee.

Thou dost know that I am praying; Thou dost know that I love no other. Yet whether Thou dost come to me or not, I will wait for Thee, though it be for eternity.

I will drive away all despondency in order to make a mighty effort to feel God by meditation, until He finally appears.

MY OFFERING TO THEE

EACH MORNING I offer my body, my mind, and any ability that I possess, to be used by Thee, O Infinite Creator, in whatever way Thou dost choose to express Thyself through me. I know that all work is Thy work, and that no task is too difficult or too menial when offered to Thee in loving service.

———— ❦ ————

Divine Mother, with the language of my soul I demand realization of Thy presence. Thou art the essence of everything. Make me see Thee in every fiber of my being, in every wisp of thought. Awaken my heart!

Beloved Father, my wordless chants of yearning for Thee will sing in cadence with my heart-throbs. I shall feel Thy presence in all hearts. I shall watch Thy hands working in the law of gravitation and in all other natural forces. In the tread of all living creatures I shall hear Thy footsteps.

Thou unseen Charmer of Souls, Thou art the fountain flowing from the bosom of friendship. Thou art the rays of secret warmth that unfold buds of feeling into blossoms of endearing, soulful words of poetry and loyalty.

As I radiate sympathy and goodwill to others I open the channel for God's love to come to me. Divine love is the magnet that attracts all blessedness.

Father, enter Thou into my soul through the portals of my heart's devotion and through my ardent prayers.

I will not become too much attached to things, as this will cause me to forget God. We lose possessions, not as a punishment, but as a test to see if we love material things more than the Infinite Lord.

I obey Thee in the temple of discipline.
I love Thee in the temple of devotion.
I worship Thee in the temple of my love.
I touch Thy feet in the temple of stillness.
I behold Thine eyes in the temple of delight.
I feel Thee in the temple of emotion.
I fight for Thee in the temple of activity.
I enjoy Thee in the temple of peace.

I will rise with the dawn and rouse my sleeping love to waken in the light of true devotion for the peace-God within.

Heavenly Father, in an invisible church built of devotion granite, receive Thou my humble heart offerings, daily renewed by prayer.

Divine Mother, open wide the bud of my devotion and release its fragrance, that it may spread from my soul to the souls of all others, ever whispering of Thee.

I HAVE HEARD THY VOICE

DIVINE MOTHER, I have heard Thy voice whispering in the fragrance of the rose. I touched Thy tenderness in the softness of the lily. In the whispers of my devotion, it was Thy love that answered.

Christ is risen from the sepulcher of my indifference, and I behold him in the light of my devotion. I, a sleeping son of God, am coming out of my bodily prison into the vast freedom of Spirit.

UNDYING DEVOTION

O THOU GREAT Lover, Thou art Life, Thou art the Goal, Thou art my Desire. Deliver me from Thy *maya** of delusion. Tempt me with Thy presence instead. Beloved Lord, fill my heart with undying devotion to Thee alone.

MY WELL OF SILENCE

HIS LAUGHTER CAUGHT my heart. His joy invaded my sorrowful heart as I swung in a hammock beneath the pines under the blue.

I felt the sky astir and His presence moving through me. My body became still; my power of silence dug into my bosom until a bottomless well sprang up.

---

* The delusive veil of creation, whose multiplicity of forms hides the One Formless Verity.

The bubbling waters of my well clamored and called all thirsty things around me to come and drink of my inspirations. Suddenly the vast blue pouted and plunged its blue lips into the well of my heart. The pines, the sailing clouds, the mountains, earth and the planets put their mouths into my well of bliss. All things in creation drank of me. Then, satisfied, they plunged into the waters of my immortality. Their gross bodies touched the transmuting pool of my soul and became purified and luminous. Just as grains of sugar dissolve in a pot of sparkling water, so the cloudlets, tall hills, scenic beauties, stars, lakes, worlds, brooklets of laughing minds, long winding rivers of ambitions of all creatures traveling along many trails of incarnations—all melted in the ocean of my all-dissolving silence.

O Divine Shepherd of Infinite Perception, rescue the lambkins of my thoughts, lost in the wilderness of restlessness, and lead them into Thy fold of silence.

Beloved Father, let the embers of my devotion glow with Thy presence evermore.

Beloved God, pluck the lotus of my devotion from the mire of earthly forgetfulness and wear it on Thy breast of ever-awake memory.

I bow to Thee, O God, in the temple of the skies, in the temple of Nature, and in the soul-temples of human brothers.

I Worship God Everywhere

I bow to the one infinite Father, differently manifesting in the many churches and temples that have all been erected in His honor. I worship the one God resting on the various altars of different teachings and religious faiths.

Today I will worship God in deep silence and wait to hear His answer through my increasing peace of meditation.

I will mingle my inner devotional whispers with the prayers of all saints, and continuously offer them in the temples of silence and activity until I can hear His whispers loudly, everywhere.

This day shall be the best day of my life. Today I will start with a new determination to dedicate my devotion forever at the feet of Omnipresence.

EXPANDING LOVE

(Meditate, dwell on, and feel this)

MY KINGDOM OF love shall expand. I have loved my body more than anything else. That is why I am identified with and limited by it. With the love that I have given to the body, I will love all those who love me. With the expanded love of those who love me, I will love those who are mine. With the love for myself and the love for my own, I will love those who are strangers. I will use all my love to love those who do not love me, as well as those who love me. I will bathe all souls in my unselfish love. In the sea of my love, my family members, my countrymen, all nations, and all beings will swim. All creation, all the myriads of tiny living things, will dance on the waves of my love.

— ❦ —

I saturate myself with the perfume of Thy presence, and I wait to waft with the breeze the aroma of Thy message of love to all.

In the temple of my earthly mother's love I will worship the incarnated love of the Divine Mother.

All desire for love I will purify and satisfy in sacred divine love for Thee, O God!

Beloved Infinite, I will keep Thee ever imprisoned behind the strong walls of my undying love.

Whether or not Thou answerest my demands and prayers, I shall go on loving Thee.

O Father, teach me to vivify my prayers with Thy love. May I realize Thy nearness behind the voice of my prayer.

I know that just behind the screen of my love-demands Thou art listening to the silent words of my soul.

I will behold God Himself bestowing on me His divine love through the hearts of all.

Naughty or good, I am Thy child. Sinner or saint, I am Thine own.

Teach me to drink the everlasting nectar of joy found in the fountain of meditation.

Divine Father, teach me to worship Thee on the altar of silence within and on the altar of activity without.

Beloved God, purify the dross in me. Banish disease and poverty from the world evermore. Banish ignorance of Thee from the shores of men's souls.

MEDITATIONS ON GOD

Meditate on God's Light

Look at a light and close your eyes. Forget the darkness around you and watch the bright red color within your eyelids. Look intently into that violet-red color. Meditate on it and imagine that it is becoming bigger and bigger. Behold around you a dimly shining sea of violet light. You are a wave of light, a ripple of peace floating on the surface of the sea.

Now watch carefully. You, the little wave, are tossing on an ocean of light. Your tiny life is a part of the all-pervading Life. As your meditation deepens, you, a little shallow wave of peace, are becoming the deep, wide ocean of peace.

Meditate on the thought, "I am a wave of peace." Feel the vastness just beneath your consciousness. The wave should feel the sustaining life of the vast ocean beneath it.

GOD'S PROTECTING PRESENCE

TEACH ME TO feel that I am enveloped always in the aureole of Thine all-protecting omnipresence, in birth, in sorrow, in joy, in activity, in meditation, in ignorance, in trials, in death, and in final emancipation.

Teach me to open the gate of meditation that alone leads to Thy blessed presence.

Behind the wave of my consciousness is the sea of cosmic consciousness. Under the ripple of my mind is the supporting ocean of Thy vastness. I am protected by Thy Divine Mind.

Thy light of goodness and Thy protective power are ever shining through me. I saw them not, because my eyes of wisdom were closed. Now Thy touch of peace has opened my eyes; Thy goodness and unfailing protection are flowing through me.

I WILL EXTOL THEE

O HEAVENLY FATHER, I will extol Thy glory, the beauties of Thy paradise within us. May I live in the garden of soul-happiness and noble thoughts and be filled with the aroma of Thy love evermore.

———❧———

O Spirit, make my soul Thy temple, but make my heart Thy beloved home where Thou wouldst dwell with me in ease and everlasting understanding.

Wilt Thou not open Thy lips of silence and whisper constant guiding thoughts to my soul?

Beloved Lord, teach me to feel that Thou art the sole activating power, and that in recognition of Thee as the Doer lies the value of all my life's experiences. Teach me to behold Thee as the only Friend, helping and encouraging me through my earthly friends.

Heavenly Father, from today I will strive to know Thee; I will make the effort to cultivate Thy friendship. All my duties will be performed with the thought that I am realizing Thee through them, and thus am pleasing Thee.

Life is a struggle for joy all along the way. May I fight to win the battle on the very spot where I now am.

When fear or anger or any kind of suffering comes to me, I will view it as a spectator. I will separate myself from my experiences. At all costs I will endeavor to retain my peace and happiness.

Beloved Father, I realize that praise does not make me any better, nor blame worse. I am what I am before my conscience and Thee. I shall travel on, doing good to all and seeking ever to please Thee, for thus shall I find my only true happiness.

TAKE THIS DARKNESS AWAY

COSMIC MOTHER, TAKE this darkness away! When I sit with eyes closed, enveloped in self-created shadows, cause Thou to blaze upon me in splendor the aurora of intuition.*

* Apprehension of knowledge derived immediately and spontaneously from the soul, not from the fallible medium of the senses or of reason.

———— ❧ ————

Mother Divine, draw aside Thy glittering veil of cosmic motion pictures and show me Thy delusion-dispersing face of mercy.

O blazing Light! awaken my heart, awaken my soul, ignite my darkness, tear the veil of silence, and fill my temple with Thy glory.

Heavenly Father, destroy in us the wrong thought of ages—that we are frail human beings. Manifest Thyself as the light behind our reason: the deep blaze of wisdom.

TEACH ME TO WORSHIP THEE

BELOVED FATHER, TEACH me the mystery of my existence! Teach me to worship Thee in breathlessness, in deathlessness. In the fire of devotion, consume my ignorance. In the stillness of my soul, come, Father, come! Possess me and make me feel, in and around me, Thine immortal presence.

In the solitude of my mind I yearn to hear Thy voice. Take away the dreams of earthly sounds that yet lurk in my memory. I want to hear Thy quiet voice ever singing in the silence of my soul.

My Lord, as Thou art omnipresent, Thou canst not but be present in me. Thou hast omnipotence and omniscience; these also are my soul attributes. May I be able to unfold even a fragment of That contained in my Self.

I WILL DRINK THY JOY

I WILL DRINK vitality from the golden fountains of sunshine; I will drink peace from the silver fountain of moonèd nights; I will drink Thy power from the mighty cup of the wind; I will drink Thy consciousness as joy and bliss from all the little cups of my thoughts.

In Thy blessed light I shall remain awake forever, watching Thy precious omnipresent face with ever vigilant eyes through all the eons of eternity.

I sought God's love in the barren dryness of mortal affection. After wandering through the desert of undependable human sympathy, at last I have found the inexhaustible oasis of divine love.

Father, teach me to reclaim my birthright and to live as an immortal.

O divine Friend! though the darkness of my ignorance be as old as the world, still make me realize that with the dawn of Thy light the darkness will vanish as though it had never been.

What is this life coursing in my veins? Could it be other than divine?

Heavenly Father, descend within me. Make me feel that Thou art present in my brain, in my spine, and in my deepest thoughts. I bow to Thee.

I am lost, Father, in the wastelands of wrong beliefs; I cannot find my home. Rise on the darkness of my mental sky and be the polestar of my groping mind. Lead me to Thyself who art my Home.

Teach me, O Christ, to redeem my mattersold mind, that I may give it to Thee in prayer and ecstasy, in meditation and reverie.

Reveal Thyself

Come Thou, O Father, reveal the vast kingdom of Thy presence! Reveal Thyself! Teach my heart to pray; teach my soul to feel that all doors may open and Thy presence be revealed.

O Cosmic Light, every day I see Thee painting the sky in bright colors. I watch Thee clothe the bare soil with green grass. Thou art in the warmth of sunshine. Oh, Thou art so plainly present everywhere! I bow to Thee.

Teach me to behold Thy face in the mirror of my stillness within.

Divine Beloved, make me know, at once and forever, that Thou hast always been mine, ever mine. My error-dreams are past, buried in the sepulcher of oblivion. I am awake, basking in the sunlight of life in Thee.

The ocean of God's abundance flows through me. I am His child. I am a channel through which all divine creative power flows. Bless me, Father, that above all things I seek Thee first, as befits Thy true child.

Beloved God, let the flowers of my devotion blossom in the garden of my heart while I await the dawn of Thy coming.

Dear Father, open all the windows of faith that I may behold Thee in the mansion of peace. Fling open the doors of silence that I may enter Thy temple of bliss.

Beloved God, protect the celestial temple of my mind against the entry of tenacious warriors of evil thoughts.

I know that I am responsible for my own welfare. Therefore I will discard all useless pursuits and idle thoughts, that daily I may find time for God.

My Heavenly Father, Thou art Love, and I am made in Thine image. I am the cosmic sphere of Love in which I behold all planets, all stars, all beings, all creation as glimmering lights. I am the Love that illumines the whole universe.

O Fountain of Love! make me feel that my heart is flooded by Thine omnipresent love.

I want Thee, O God, that I may give Thee to all!

Father of Hearts, awaken eternally the consciousness of Thy loving presence within me.

Divine Father, teach me to dive again and again into meditation, deeper and deeper, until I find Thine immortal pearls of wisdom and divine joy.

On the throne of silent thoughts the God of peace is directing my actions today. I will usher my brothers into the temple of God through the door of my peace.

Whether I am a small or a big wave of being, the same Ocean of Life is behind me.

I will think until I find the ultimate answer. I will turn the power of thought into a searchlight whose brightness will reveal the face of Omnipresence.

Teach me to think of Thee until Thou dost become my only thought.

O Father, no matter what my tests be, may I bear them joyously by feeling Thy presence always in my heart. Thus all the tragedies and comedies of life will seem naught but dramas of ecstatic entertainment.

Father, transfer my consciousness from my limitations, suggested by others and by my own weak thoughts, to the realization that I, Thy child, am the owner of Thy kingdom of infinite possessions.

O Fountain of Flame, let Thy light be established within me, about me, everywhere.

A true yogi feels the throb of his heart in all hearts; his mind in all minds; his presence in all motion. I will be a true yogi.

O Father, show me the highway that leads to Thee. Give me bursting aspirations of the heart. In the echo of devotion teach me to hear Thy voice.

In the stillness of my soul I humbly bow before Thine omnipresence, knowing that Thou art ever leading me onward and upward on the path of Self-realization.

O Lord, Thy love flowing through human hearts has lured me to find the source of perfect love in Thee.

Divine Spirit, I will seek Thee until I find Thee. Finding Thee I will reverently receive whatever gifts it is Thy desire I should have. But I ask nothing throughout eternity save the complete gift of Thyself.

I come to Thee with folded hands, bowed head, and heart laden with the myrrh of reverence.

Thou art my Parents; I am Thy child. Thou art the Master; I will obey the silent command of Thy voice.

EXPANSION OF CONSCIOUSNESS

TUNE IN WITH THE COSMIC SOUND

LISTEN TO THE cosmic sound of *Aum,* a great hum of countless atoms, in the sensitive right side of your head. This is the voice of God. Feel the sound spreading through the brain. Hear its continuous pounding roar.

Now hear and feel it surging into the spine, bursting open the doors of the heart. Feel it resounding through every tissue, every feeling, every cord of your nerves. Every blood cell, every thought is dancing on the sea of roaring vibration.

Observe the spreading volume of the cosmic sound. It sweeps through the body and mind into the earth and the surrounding atmosphere. You are moving with it, into the airless ether, and into millions of universes of matter.

Meditate on the marching spread of the cosmic sound. It has passed through the physical universes to the subtle shining veins of rays that hold all matter in manifestation.

The cosmic sound is commingling with millions of multicolored rays. The cosmic sound has entered the realm of cosmic rays. Listen to, behold, and feel the embrace of the cosmic sound and the eternal light. The cosmic sound now pierces through the heart-fires of cosmic energy and they both melt within the ocean of cosmic consciousness and cosmic joy. The body melts into the universe. The universe melts into the soundless voice. The sound melts into the all-shining light. And the light enters the bosom of infinite joy.

THE COSMIC SEA

WHEN YOU FIND that your soul, your heart, every wisp of inspiration, every speck of the vast blue sky and its shining star-blossoms, the mountains, the earth, the whippoorwill, and the bluebells are all tied together with one cord of rhythm, one cord of joy, one cord of unity, one cord of Spirit, then you shall know that all are but waves in His cosmic sea.

I GO WITHIN

I WAS A prisoner carrying a heavy load of bones and flesh, but I have broken the chains of my muscle-bound body by the power of relaxation. I am free. Now I shall try to go within.

Bewitching scenic beauties, stop your dance

before my eyes! Lure not my attention away!

Enchanting melodies, keep not my mind enthralled in the revels of earthly songs!

Haunting sirens of sweet sensations, paralyze not my sacred intuitions by your enticing touch! Let my meditation race for the sweet bower of eternal divine love.

Luring aroma of lilacs, jasmine, and roses, stop not my homeward-marching mind!

These tempting enchantresses of the senses are now gone. The cords of flesh are broken. The grip of the senses is loosened. I exhale and stop the storm of breath; the ripples of thought melt away.

I am sitting on the altar of my throbbing heart. I watch the roaring, shouting torrent of life-force moving through the heart into the body. I turn backward to the spine. The beat and roar of the heart are gone. Like a sacred hidden river my life-force flows in the gorge of the spine. I enter a dim corridor through the door of the spiritual eye, and speed on until at last the river of my life flows into the ocean of Life and loses itself in bliss.

God's vastness I glimpsed in the skies of quietness. His joy I tasted in the fountains of my existence. His voice I heard in my un-sleeping conscience.

I will consciously receive the light of the omnipresent Father constantly passing through me.

O Father, break the boundaries of the little waves of my life that I may join the ocean of Thy vastness.

EXPANSION IN ETERNITY

ETERNITY YAWNS AT me below, above, on the left and on the right, in front and behind, within and without.

With open eyes I behold myself as the little body. With closed eyes I perceive myself as the cosmic center around which revolves the sphere of eternity, the sphere of bliss, the sphere of omniscient, living space.

I feel the Lord like a gentle breath of bliss breathing in my body of universes. I perceive Him shining through the bright twinkles of all luminosity and through the waves of cosmic consciousness.

I behold Him as the light of solar inspiration holding the luminaries of my thoughts in the rhythms of balance.

I feel Him as a bursting voice, leading,

guiding, teaching secretly in the soul temples of all men and all creation.

He is the fountain of wisdom and of radiant inspiration flowing through all souls. He is the fragrance oozing from the incense vase of all hearts. He is a garden of celestial blossoms and bright thought-flowers. He is the love that inspires our love-dreams.

I feel Him percolating through my heart, as through all hearts, through the pores of the earth, through the sky, through all created things. He is the eternal motion of joy. He is the mirror of silence in which all creation is reflected.

My earthly experiences serve as a process of destruction of my limiting mortal delusions. In God even the most "impossible" dreams are realized. ("I will give him the morning star."—Revelation 2:28.)

I am submerged in Thine eternal light; it permeates every particle of my being. I am living in that light. Divine Spirit, I behold only Thee, within and without.

I will close my physical eyes and dismiss the temptations of matter. I will peer through the darkness of silence until my eyes of relativity open into the one inner eye of light. When my two eyes that behold both good and evil become single, and behold in everything only the divine goodness of God, I shall see that my body, mind, and soul have become filled with His omnipresent light.

The reality of my life cannot die, for I am indestructible consciousness.

All the veils of my ignorant outer life are burned in the light of my awakening in Christ, and I behold the Intelligence of the baby Jesus cradled in the petals of roses, in the weaving of lights, and in the love thoughts of all true hearts.

I am infinite. I am spaceless, I am tireless; I am beyond body, thought, and utterance; beyond all matter and mind. I am endless bliss.

The ocean of Spirit has become the little bubble of my soul. Whether floating in birth, or disappearing in death, in the ocean of cosmic awareness the bubble of my life cannot die. I am indestructible consciousness, protected in the bosom of Spirit's immortality.

I am no longer the wave of consciousness thinking itself separated from the sea of cosmic consciousness. I am the ocean of Spirit that has become the wave of human life.

Like a silent invisible river flowing beneath the desert flows the vast dimensionless river of Spirit, through the sands of time, through the sands of experience, through the sands of all souls, through the sands of all living atoms, through the sands of all space.

O Father, Thou art sacred perennial joy, Thou art the joy I seek, Thou art the joy of the soul. Teach me to worship Thee through the joy born of meditation.

THE HOLY SOUND OF AUM

TEACH ME TO hear Thy voice, O Father, the cosmic voice that commanded all vibration to spring forth. Manifest to me as *Aum,* the cosmic song of all sound.

O Holy Ghost, sacred *Aum* vibration, enlarge my consciousness as I listen to thine omnipresent sound. Make me feel that I am both the cosmic ocean and the little wave of body-vibration in it.

O omnipresent cosmic sound of *Aum,* reverberate through me, expanding my consciousness from the body to the universe, and teach me to feel in Thee the all-permeating perennial bliss.

O infinite Energy, infinite Wisdom, recharge me with Thy spiritual vibration.

O cosmic sound of *Aum,* guide me, be with me, lead me from darkness to light.

I AM FLYING HOME

GOOD-BYE, BLUE house of heaven. Farewell, stars and celestial celebrities and your dramas on the screen of space. Good-bye, flowers with your traps of beauty and fragrance. You can hold me no longer. I am flying Home.

Adieu to the warm embrace of sunshine. Farewell, cool, soothing, comforting breeze. Good-bye, entertaining music of man.

I stayed long reveling with all of you, dancing with my variously costumed thoughts, drinking the wine of my feelings and my mundane will. I have now forsaken the intoxications of delusion.

Good-bye, muscles, bones, and bodily motions. Farewell, breath. I cast thee away from my breast. Adieu, heartthrobs, emotions, thoughts, and memories. I am flying Home in a plane of silence. I go to feel my heartthrob in Him.

I soar in the plane of consciousness above, beneath, on the left, on the right, within and without, everywhere, to find that in every nook of my space-home I have always been in the sacred presence of my Father.

I Am in All Places

I AM BEHOLDING through the eyes of all. I am working through all hands, I am walking through all feet. The brown, white, olive, yellow, red, and black bodies are all mine.

I am thinking with the minds of all, I am dreaming through all dreams, I am feeling through all feelings. The flowers of joy blooming on all heart-tracts are mine.

I am eternal laughter. My smiles are dancing through all faces. I am the waves of enthusiasm in all God-tuned hearts.

I am the wind of wisdom that dries the sighs and sorrows of all humanity. I am the silent joy of life moving through all beings.

Heavenly Father, teach me to find freedom in Thee, that I may know nothing on earth belongs to me; all belongs only to Thee. Teach me to know my home is Thine omnipresence.

O Cosmic Silence, I hear Thy voice through the murmur of brooks, the song of the nightingale, the sounding of conch shells, the beat of ocean waves, and the hum of vibrations.

Beloved God, no more with words but with the burning flame of my heart's love I worship Thee.

Teach me to behold Thy vastness, Thy changelessness behind all things, that I may perceive myself as a part of Thy changeless Being.

O mighty Ocean, I pray that the rivers of my desires, meandering through many deserts of difficulties, may merge at last in Thee.

I will conflagrate all space and roll over its bosom, unburnt and deathless. I will dive into infinity, never reaching the end. I will run and race and spread my laughter in all things, in all motion, and in the motionless void.

Awaken me, O Heavenly Father, that I may arise from the confining tomb of flesh into the consciousness of my cosmic body.

O immortal Love, unite my love with Thy love, unite my life with Thy joy, and my mind with Thy cosmic consciousness.

Let me behold naught but beauty, naught

but good, naught but truth, naught but Thine immortal fountain of bliss.

In the hall of creation, O Divine Mother, everywhere I hear the rhythm of Thy foot-steps, dancing wildly in the booming thunder and softly in the song of atoms.

EXPLANATION OF "AUM" AND "CHRIST CONSCIOUSNESS"

In *Autobiography of a Yogi* Paramahansa Yogananda says: "*The Comforter, which is the Holy Ghost, whom the Father will send in my name, he shall teach you all things, and bring all things to your remembrance, what-soever I have said to you*' (John 14:26). These bibli-cal words refer to the threefold nature of God as Father, Son, Holy Ghost (*Sat, Tat, Aum* in the Hindu scriptures).

"God the Father is the Absolute, Unmanifested, existing *beyond* vibratory creation. God the Son is the Christ Consciousness existing *within* vibratory creation; this Christ Consciousness is the 'only begotten' or sole reflection of the Uncreated Infinite.

"The outward manifestation of the omnipresent Christ Consciousness, its 'witness' (Revelation 3:14), is *Aum* (*Om*), the Word or Holy Ghost: invisible divine power, the only doer, the sole causative and activating force that upholds all creation through vibration. *Aum* the blissful Comforter is heard in meditation and reveals to the devotee the ultimate Truth, bringing 'all things to your remembrance.'"

ON FINDING GOD

ON SPREADING RIPPLES OF PEACE

FIX YOUR MIND inwardly between the eye-brows on the shoreless lake of peace. Watch the eternal circle of rippling peace around you. The more you watch intently, the more you will feel the wavelets of peace spreading from the eyebrows to the forehead, from the forehead to the heart, and on to every cell in your body. Now the waters of peace are over-flowing the banks of your body and inundating the vast territory of your mind. The flood of peace flows over the boundaries of your mind and moves on in infinite directions.

With the sword of peace, O Lord, let me fight through the thick skirmish of trials.

I am the prince of perpetual peace playing in a drama of sad and happy dreams on the stage of experience.

PEACE

Peace flows through my heart, and blows through me as a zephyr.

Peace fills me like a fragrance.

Peace runs through me like rays.

Peace stabs the heart of noise and worries.

Peace burns through my disquietude.

Peace, like a globe of fire, expands and fills my omnipresence.

Peace, like an ocean, rolls on in all space.

Peace, like red blood, vitalizes the veins of my thoughts.

Peace, like a boundless aureole, encircles my body of infinity.

Peace-flames blow through the pores of my

flesh, and through all space.

The perfume of peace flows over the gardens
of blossoms.

The wine of peace runs perpetually through
the winepress of all hearts.

Peace is the breath of stones, stars, and sages.

Peace is the ambrosial wine of Spirit flowing
from the cask of silence,

Which I quaff with my countless mouths of
atoms.

MEDITATION ON SILENCE

MY SILENCE, LIKE an expanding sphere, spreads
everywhere.

My silence spreads like a radio song, above,
beneath, left and right, within and without.

My silence spreads like a wildfire of bliss;
the dark thickets of sorrow and the tall oaks of

pride are all burning up.

My silence, like the ether, passes through everything, carrying the songs of earth, atoms, and stars into the halls of His infinite mansion.

Let me not drug myself with the opiate of restlessness. Beneath the throb of my heart may I feel the presence of God's peace.

I will fill my heart with the peace of meditation. I will pour heartfuls of my joy into peace-thirsty souls.

All spiritually successful persons, such as Jesus, Babaji, Lahiri Mahasaya, Sri Yukteswar, Swami Shankara, and other masters are manifestations of our one Father, God. I am happy in the thought that my spiritual ambition to realize unity with God is one that has already been attained by all great masters.

Each day I will meditate more deeply than yesterday. Each tomorrow I will meditate more deeply than today. I will meditate during most of my leisure hours.

O Lord, with the soft touch of intuition I will tune my soul radio and rid my mind of static restlessness, that I may hear Thy voice of cosmic vibration, the music of atoms, and the melody of love vibrating in my super-consciousness.

Today I will seek Thee, O Father, as the ever-increasing bliss of meditation. I will feel Thee as boundless joy throbbing in my heart. Finding Thee, I shall find all things I crave through Thee.

Teach me to find Thy presence on the altar of my constant peace and in the joy that springs from deep meditation.

Bless me, that I may find Thee in the temple of each thought and activity. Finding Thee within, I shall find Thee without, in all people and all conditions.

Teach me to feel that it is Thy smile manifesting in the dawn, on the lips of roses, and on the faces of noble men and women.

GOD'S FLAMING PRESENCE

I WILL DO away with the mockery of parroting prayer. I will pray deeply until the darkness of meditation burns with Thy flaming presence.

Heavenly Father, I cannot wait until to-morrow for Thy song. Today I will broadcast my soul-call into the ether with such loving concentration that Thou must respond through the receiver of my silence.

O Spirit! ever-existing, ever-conscious, ever-new Bliss! Take away from my mind the weight of indifference and forgetfulness. May I drink the nectar of Thine ever blessed presence.

With the deepening of inner and outer silence, Thy peace comes to me. I will try always to hear the echo of Thy footsteps.

Having Thee as the deepest joy of deepest meditation, I know that all things — prosperity, health, and wisdom — will be added unto me.

Teach me to fish for Thee in the deepest waters of my soul.

FIND GOD IN JOY

NO MATTER WHAT causes it, whenever a little bubble of joy appears in your invisible sea of consciousness, take hold of it, and keep expanding it. Meditate on it and it will grow larger. Watch not the limitations of the little bubble of your joy, but keep expanding it until it grows bigger and bigger. Keep puffing at it with the breath of concentration from within, until it spreads all over the ocean of infinity in your consciousness. Keep puffing at the bubble of joy until it breaks its confining walls and becomes the sea of joy.

In the sound of the viol, the flute, and the deep-toned organ I hear God's voice.

Within the soul is the joy that my ego is seeking. I suddenly become aware of His bliss honeycombed in the hive of silence. I will break the hive of secret silence and drink the honey of unceasing blessedness.

MY BELOVED IS CALLING ME

WITH FLOWERS, WITH bright skies, with the divine manna of joy in happy minds, with souls full of wisdom, with songs of the birds, with divine melodies in the hearts of men, my Beloved is calling me to retrace my footsteps to His home of peace within.

I will seek the kingdom of God in the joy arising from constant, long, deep, continuous meditation. I will conscientiously seek to find the Lord within, and will not be satisfied with the little imaginary inspirations that come from short, restless silences. I will meditate more and more deeply until I feel His presence.

By realizing God I shall be reclaimed as His child. Without asking or begging I shall receive all prosperity, health, and wisdom.

O Thou Perfume of all hearts and all roses, I mind not how many days of scalding sorrow cross the threshold of my life to search and test me. Through Thy blessing may they re-mind me of my errors that have kept me away from Thee.

Protector of All, I care not if all things else

are wrested away from me by my self-created destiny; but I shall demand of Thee, mine Own, to guard the slender taper of my love for Thee.

O glorious Omnipresence, let not the fire of memory for Thee be blown out by the gusts of oblivion arising from the whirlwinds of my worldliness.

Through meditation I will stop the storm of breath, mental restlessness, and sensory disturbances raging over the lake of my mind. Through prayer and meditation I will harness my will and activity to the right goal.

MY OMNIPRESENT THRONE

I CAME DOWN from my omnipresent throne of love in the bosom of space and in the hearts of twinkling lights to find a cozy place in the heart of man. I stayed there long, shut out from my large, large home.

I was everywhere; then I hid myself away in the small places. Now I come out of my hiding places. I open the gates of the human limitations of family, caste, color, and creed. I am racing everywhere to feel again my consciousness of omnipresence.

Through the transparency of my deepest meditation I shall receive the light of the omnipresent Father passing through me.

The moment I am restless or disturbed in mind, I will retire to silence and meditation until calmness is restored. I will begin each day with concentration and meditation on the Supreme Being.

MEDITATIONS ON THE CHRIST

I WILL FOLLOW the shepherds of faith, devotion, and meditation. Guided by the star of soul wisdom, the shepherds will lead me to the Christ.

I will behold the "only begotten," the sole reflection of transcendental God the Father, born in the womb of finite vibratory matter as the Christ Intelligence that shepherds all creation to an intelligent divine end.

I will break the chains of restlessness and will limitlessly expand the power of my meditation until the universal Christ Consciousness is able to manifest fully through me.

Bless me, Father, that the single eye of realization lead me to behold through all the veils of matter the infinite presence of Christ.

I Will Meditate

BELOVED GOD, SINCE no earthly engagement is possible without my using powers received from Thee, I will renounce everything that interferes with my daily engagement to meditate on Thee.

Today I will meditate no matter how tired I think I feel. I will not allow myself to be a victim of distracting noise while trying to meditate. I will transfer my consciousness to the inner world.

Through the gateway of meditation I will enter God's temple of peace everlasting. There I will worship Him at the altar of ever new contentment. I will kindle the fire of happiness to illuminate His temple within.

I will meditate regularly, that the light of faith may usher me into the immortal kingdom of my Heavenly Father.

Divine Mother, I will pull away the starry veil of the blue, I will tear away the cover of space, I will melt away the magic carpet of thoughts, I will shut off the diverting motion pictures of life, that I may behold Thee.

I know God can be realized through meditation, by intuitional perception, but not by the restless mind.

I will open my eyes to the joy of meditation; then I shall see all darkness vanish.

I will bathe in the sacred pool of God's love hidden behind the ramparts of meditation.

I will make my inner environment perfect through meditation, that it be impervious to all adverse outside influences.

I will begin each day with meditation on the Supreme Being.

In the temple of silence I discover Thine altar of peace. On the altar of peace I find Thine ever new joy.

Let me hear Thy voice, O God, in the cave of meditation. I will find perpetual celestial happiness within. Then peace will reign in my heart whether I am in silence or in the midst of activities.

Every star of heaven, every pure thought, every good act shall be a window through which to behold Thee.

With infinite concentration and devotion pour your consciousness through the spiritual eye into Infinitude. Release your soul from the imprisonment of the body into the vast ocean of Spirit.

ON MATERIAL CONCERNS

NEVER LOSE HOPE

IF YOU HAVE given up hope of ever being happy, cheer up. Never lose hope. Your soul, being a reflection of the ever joyous Spirit, is, in essence, happiness itself.

If you keep the eyes of your concentration closed, you cannot see the sun of happiness burning within your bosom; but no matter how tightly you close the eyes of your attention, the fact nevertheless remains that the happiness rays are ever trying to pierce the closed doors of your mind. Open the windows of calmness and you will find a sudden burst of the bright sun of joy within your very Self.

The joyous rays of the soul may be perceived if you interiorize your attention. These perceptions may be had by training your mind to enjoy the beautiful scenery of thoughts in the invisible, intangible kingdom within you. Do not search for happiness only in beautiful clothes, clean houses, delicious dinners, soft cushions, and luxuries. These will imprison your happiness behind the bars of externality, of outwardness. Rather, in the airplane of your visualization, glide over the limitless empire of thoughts. There behold the mountain ranges of unbroken, lofty, spiritual aspirations for improving yourself and others.

Glide over the deep valleys of universal sympathy. Fly over the geysers of enthusiasm, over the Niagara Falls of perpetual wisdom, plunging down the hoary crags of your soul's peace. Soar over the endless river of intuitive perception to the kingdom of His omnipresence.

There, in His mansion of bliss, drink from His fountain of whispering wisdom, and quench the thirst of your desire. Dine with Him on the fruits of divine love in the banquet hall of eternity. If you have made up your mind to find joy within yourself, sooner or later you shall find it. Seek it now, daily, by steady, deeper and deeper meditation within. Make a true effort to go within and you will find there your longed-for happiness.

THE LIGHT OF SMILES

(Meditate, dwell on, and practice this daily)

I WILL LIGHT the match of smiles. My gloom veil will disappear. I shall behold my soul in the light of my smiles, hidden behind the accumulated darkness of ages. When I find myself, I shall race through all hearts with the torch of my soul-smiles. My heart will smile first, then my eyes and my face. Every body-part will shine in the light of smiles.

I will run amid the thickets of melancholy hearts and make a bonfire of all sorrows. I am the irresistible fire of smiles. I will fan myself with the breeze of God-joy and blaze my way through the darkness of all minds. My smiles will convey His smiles and whoever meets me will catch a whiff of my divine joy. I will carry fragrant purifying torches of smiles for all hearts.

I will help weeping ones to smile, by smiling myself, even when it is difficult.

In the cheer of all hearts I hear the echo of Thy bliss. In the friendship of all true hearts I discover Thy friendship. I rejoice as much in the prosperity of my brothers as I do in my own prosperity. In helping others to be wise I increase my own wisdom. In the happiness of all I find my own happiness.

Nothing shall blight my smiles. Grim death, disease, or failure cannot daunt me. Disaster cannot really touch me, for within my soul I possess the unconquerable, unchangeable, ever new bliss of God.

O divine silent Laughter, be enthroned beneath the canopy of my countenance and smile through my soul.

I will try to be a joy billionaire, finding my wealth in the coin of Thy realm — ever new bliss. Thus I shall satisfy my need for spiritual and material prosperity at the same time.

SPREADING DIVINE JOY

BEGINNING WITH THE early dawn each day, I will radiate joy to everyone I meet. I will be mental sunshine for all who cross my path. I will burn candles of smiles in the bosoms of the joyless. Before the unfading light of my cheer, darkness will take flight.

Let my love spread its laughter in all hearts, in every person belonging to every race. Let my love rest in the hearts of flowers, of animals, and of little specks of stardust.

I will try to be happy under all circumstances. I will make up my mind to be happy within myself right now, where I am today.

Let my soul smile through my heart and let my heart smile through my eyes, that I may scatter Thy rich smiles in sad hearts.

I will always behold in my life the perfect, healthy, all-wise, all-blissful image of God.

HEALING LIGHT OF GOD

THY PERFECT LIGHT is omnipresent in all my body parts. Wherever that healing light is manifest, there is perfection. I am well, for perfection is in me.

Thy healing light has been shining within me, around me, but I kept the eyes of my inner perceptions closed and beheld not Thy transmuting light.

I will plunge the gaze of my faith through the window of the spiritual eye and baptize my body in the healing light of Christ Consciousness.

Heavenly Father, teach me to remember Thee in poverty or prosperity, in sickness or health, in ignorance or wisdom. Teach me to open my closed eyes of unbelief and behold Thine instantaneously healing light.

FOR HEALTH AND VITALITY

TODAY I WILL seek God's vitality in the sun, bathing my body in its light to appreciate the life-giving, disease-destroying gift of the ultraviolet rays from the Lord.

Heavenly Father, my body cells are made of light, my fleshly cells are made of Thee.

They are Spirit, for Thou art Spirit; they are immortal, for Thou art Life.

The light of Thy perfect health permeates the dark nooks of my bodily sickness. In all my body cells Thy healing light is shining. They are entirely well, for Thy perfection is in them.

I recognize my illness to be the result of my transgression against health laws. I will undo the evil by right eating, exercise, and right thinking.

With faith in my Father I behold the shadows of sickness obliterated now and forever. I fully realize that His light exists always; I may not be overwhelmed by my self-created darkness, except when I willfully close my eyes of wisdom.

Father, help me, that I may naturally, spontaneously, and easily form the habit of proper eating. May I never become a victim of greed and thus cause myself suffering.

Heavenly Father, charge my body with Thy vitality, charge my mind with Thy spiritual power, charge my soul with Thy joy, Thine immortality.

Heavenly Father, fill my veins with Thine invisible rays, making me strong and tireless.

The all-seeing eye is behind my eyes. They are strong, for Thou dost see through them.

I AM NOT THE BODY

BELOVED GOD, I know that I am not the body, not the blood, not the energy, not the thoughts, not the mind, not the ego, not the astral self. I am the immortal soul that illumines them all, remaining unchangeable in spite of their changes.

Eternal Youth of body and mind, abide in me forever, forever, forever.

More and more I will depend for energy upon the limitless supply of the inner source of cosmic consciousness, and less and less upon outer sources of body energy.

O Father, Thine unlimited and all-healing power is in me. Manifest Thy light through the darkness of my ignorance.

O Spirit, teach me to heal the body by recharging it with Thy cosmic energy; to heal the mind by concentration and smiles.

To Broadcast to Others

FIX THE GAZE of your restless eyes on the spot between the eyebrows. Dive into the sacred star of meditation.* Keep broadcasting love thoughts to your dear ones of this world and to those who have gone ahead of you in robes of light.

There is no space between minds and souls, though their physical vehicles may be far apart.

* "During deep meditation, the single or spiritual eye (variously referred to in scriptures as the third eye, the star of the East, etc.) becomes visible within the central part of the forehead. The will, projected from this point, is the *broadcasting* apparatus of thought. Man's feeling or emotional power, calmly concentrated on the heart, enables it to act as a mental radio that *receives* the messages of other persons, far or near."—*Autobiography of a Yogi*

In thought our loved ones are really ever near.

Keep broadcasting, "I am happy in the happiness of my dear ones who are on earth or in the great beyond."

I will seek the kingdom of God first, and make sure of my actual oneness with Him. Then, if it be His will, all things—wisdom, abundance, and health—will be added unto me as part of my divine birthright, since He made me in His image.

Father, I have been like the prodigal son. I have wandered away from Thy home of all power, but now I am back in Thy home of Self-realization. I want the good things that Thou hast, for they all belong to me. I am Thy child.

I am an image of the supreme Spirit. My Father possesses everything. I and my Father are one. Having the Father, I have everything. I own everything that He owns.

Heavenly Father, I now realize that all the pursuits of a material life, even though crowned with fulfillment, offer only temporary joy. In oneness with Thee I shall find the reservoir of perennial bliss.

FRIENDSHIP AND SERVICE

I WILL ABIDE in receptive hearts—an unknown friend, ever rousing them to sacred feelings, silently urging them through their own noble thoughts to forsake their slumber of earthliness. In the light of wisdom I will dance with all their joys in the unseen bower of silence.

I will behold the person who now considers himself as my enemy to be in truth my divine brother hiding behind a veil of misunderstanding. I will tear aside this veil with a dagger of love so that, seeing my humble, forgiving understanding, he will no longer spurn the offering of my goodwill.

The door of my friendliness will ever be open equally for those brothers who hate me and for those who love me.

I will feel for others as I feel for myself. I will work out my own salvation by serving my fellowman.

I know that if I offer my friendship to all, as Christ did, I shall begin to feel the cosmic love, which is God. Human friendship is the echo of God's friendship. The greatest thing that Jesus Christ demonstrated was giving love in return for hatred. To give hatred for hatred is easy, but to give love for hatred is more difficult and far greater. Therefore I will consume hatred in the roaring conflagration of my spreading love.

I will take the best from every people. I will admire the good qualities of all nationalities and will not put my attention on their errors.

This day I will break the boundaries of self-love and of family loves and make my heart big enough for all God's children. I will kindle a fire of universal love, beholding my Heavenly Father dwelling in the temple of all natural ties. All desire for affection I will purify and satisfy in attaining the sacred love of God.

I WILL SERVE ALL

O BESTOWER OF unceasing bliss! I will seek to make others truly happy, in gratitude for the divine joy Thou hast given me. Through my spiritual happiness I will serve all.

Today I forgive all those who have ever offended me. I give my love to all thirsty hearts, both to those who love me and to those who do not love me.

I will be a fisher of souls. I will catch the ignorance of others in a net of my wisdom and offer it for transmutation to the God of all gods.

I will radiate love and goodwill to others, that I may open a channel for God's love to come to all.

I know I am one with the light of Thy goodness. May I be a lighthouse for those who are tossed on the sea of sorrow.

I am the servant ready to serve all needy minds with my simple advice, with my gifts of healing truth, and with my humble wisdom gathered in the shrine of silence. My highest ambition is to establish a temple of soul silence in every person I meet.

DIVINE PROSPERITY

THE KING OF the universe is my Father. I am the prince-successor to all His kingdom of power, wealth, and wisdom.

Falling into a forgetful state of mortal beggary, I have failed to claim my divine birthright.

O Father, I want prosperity, health, and wisdom without measure, not from earthly sources but from Thine all-possessing, all-powerful, all-bountiful hands.

I will not be a beggar, asking limited mortal prosperity, health, and knowledge. I am Thy child, and as such I demand, without limitations, a divine son's share of Thine illimitable riches.

Father, let me feel that I am Thy child. Save me from beggary! Let all good things, including health, prosperity, and wisdom, seek me instead of my pursuing them.

Lord, teach me to remember and be grateful for the years of health I have enjoyed.

I will spend less and less, not like a miser, but as a man of self-control. I will spend less that I may save more, and with those savings bring material security to myself and my family. I will also liberally help my needy human brothers.

The kingdom of the planets and all the riches of the earth belong to Thee, my Divine Father. I am Thy child; therefore I am the owner of all things even as Thou art.

Father, teach me to include the prosperity of others in the pursuit of my own prosperity.

THE ONE IN ALL

I WILL BEHOLD the Invisible in the visible forms of my father, mother, and friends, sent here to love and help me. I will show my love for God by loving them all. In their human expressions of affection I will recognize only the One Divine Love.

I bow to the Christ in the temples of all human brothers, in the temple of all life.

O Father, teach me to feel that Thou art the power behind all wealth, and the value within all things. Finding Thee first, I will find everything else in Thee.

Wherever people appreciate my efforts to do good, I shall know that there is the place where I can be of greatest service.

O Lord of Law, since all affairs are directly or indirectly guided by Thy will, I will bring Thy presence consciously into my mind through meditation, in order to solve the problems life has sent me.

God is peace. Resign yourself to the infinite peace within you. God is the ever new joy of meditation. Resign yourself to the great love within you.

O Infinite One, forever show Thy glowing face in all my joys and in the flaming light of my love for Thee.

Teach me to know that Thou art the power that keeps me healthy, prosperous, and seeking Thy truth.

I am a spark from the Infinite. I am not flesh and bones. I am light.

In helping others to succeed I shall find my own prosperity. In the welfare of others I shall find my own well-being.

ON SELF-IMPROVEMENT

MEDITATING ON THE MOONBEAMS

MIX YOUR MIND with the moonbeams at night. Wash your sorrows in their rays. Feel the mystic light spreading silently over your body, over trees, over vast lands. Standing in an open space with quiet eyes, behold, beyond the limits of the moonbeam-revealed scenery, the bedimmed fringe of the shining horizon. Let your mind, by steady wing-beats of meditation, spread beyond the lines of visible scenes and over the horizon. Let your meditation run past the rim of the visible to the lands of fancy.

Spread your mind from the moonbeam-visible objects to the dim stars and distant skies lying beyond in the eternal stillness of the ether, all throbbing with life. Watch the moonbeams spread, not only on one side of the earth, but everywhere in the eternal region of your spacious mind. Meditate until, in the cool moonbeams of your calmness, you race over trackless skies and, in realization, behold the universe as Light.

ATTAINING FREEDOM

WHY TIE THE infinite soul to a bony post of flesh? Let go! Cut the cords of flesh consciousness, attachments to the body, hunger, pleasure, pain, and bodily and mental involvements. Relax. Loosen the soul from the grip of the body. Let not the heaving breath remind you of physical bars. Sit still in breathless silence, expecting every minute to make the dash for freedom into the Infinite. Love not your earthly prison.

Free mind from body with a keen-edged

knife of stillness. Cut loose your consciousness from the body. Use it no more as an excuse to accept limitations. Turn away your consciousness from the binding body-post. Rush your consciousness beyond the body, sweeping through the minds, hearts, and souls of others. Switch on your light in all lives. Feel that you are the One Life that shines in all creation.

CREATIVE ACTIVITY

I WILL USE my creative thinking ability to gain success in every worthwhile project that I undertake. God will help me if I also try to help myself.

I have buried dead disappointments in the cemeteries of yesterday. Today I will plow the garden of life with my new creative efforts. Therein I will sow seeds of wisdom, health, prosperity, and happiness. I will water them with self-confidence and faith, and will wait for the Divine to give me the rightful harvest.

If I reap not the harvest, I will be thankful for the satisfaction of having tried my best. I will thank God that I am able to try again and again, until with His help I do succeed. I will thank Him when I have succeeded in fulfilling my heart's worthy desire.

I will try to perform only dutiful, noble actions to please God.

I am the captain of my ship of good judgment, will, and activity. I will guide my ship of life, ever beholding the polestar of His peace shining in the firmament of my deep meditation.

I will be calmly active, actively calm. I will not become lazy and mentally ossified. Nor will I be overactive, able to earn money but unable to enjoy life. I will meditate regularly to maintain true balance.

Today I open the door of my calmness and let the footsteps of Silence gently enter the temple of all my activities. I will perform all duties serenely, saturated with peace.

As I work and exercise my powers of creativity I will remember that it is Thou who art working and creating through me.

Working for God

I WILL ACQUIRE divinely deep, God-given concentration, and then use its unlimited power to meet all demands of my life.

I will do everything with deep attention: my work at home, in the office, in the world—all duties great and small will be performed well.

On the throne of silent thoughts the God of peace is directing my actions today.

After contacting God in meditation I will go about my work, whatever it may be, knowing that He is with me, directing me and giving me power to bring forth that for which I am striving.

I will use my money to make the world family better and happier, according to the measure of my ability.

OVERCOMING FEAR AND WORRY

GOD IS WITHIN me, around me, protecting me, so I will banish the gloom of fear that shuts out His guiding light and makes me stumble into ditches of error.

I will wipe away, with the soothing veil of Divine Mother's peace, the dream fears of disease, sadness, and ignorance.

Teach me to be tenaciously and cautiously courageous instead of often being afraid.

I am protected behind the battlements of my good conscience. I have burned my past. I am interested only in today.

I will fear nothing except myself, when I try to deceive my conscience.

Today I will burn the fagots of worries and fears, and kindle the fire of happiness to illumine God's temple within.

Father, teach me not to torture myself and others with the ugly fires of jealousy. Teach me to accept with satisfaction the measure of kindness and friendship from my loved ones that I deserve. Teach me not to moan for what I may not receive. Teach me to use love instead of jealousy to rouse others to do their duty toward me.

As the sun spreads vital rays of light, I will spread rays of hope in the hearts of the poor and forsaken, and kindle a new strength in the hearts of those who think that they are failures.

I will seek divine safety first, last, and all the time in the constant underlying thought of God, my greatest Friend and Protector.

Heavenly Spirit, bless me that I may easily find happiness instead of becoming worried at every test and difficulty.

OVERCOMING ANGER

I MAKE UP my mind never more to wear anger on my face. I will not inject the poison of anger in the heart of my peace and thus kill my spiritual life.

I will be angry only with anger and with

nothing else. I cannot be angry with anyone because the good and the bad both are divine brethren, born of my one divine Father.

I will calm the wrath of others by the good example of my tranquillity, especially when I see my brothers suffering from the delirium of anger.

Teach me not to kindle anger and thus devastate with the conflagration of wrath the green oasis of peace within me and in others. Teach me rather to extinguish anger with the torrents of my unceasing love.

Heavenly Father, command the lake of my kindness ever to remain undisturbed by the storms of misery-making anger.

On Criticism and Misunderstanding

I WILL NOT waste my time in talking about the faults of others. If I find myself inclined to enjoy criticizing others I will first talk loudly against myself before others.

I will criticize no one unless asked by him to do so, and then only with a desire to help.

I will try to please everyone by kind, considerate actions, ever striving to remove any misunderstanding knowingly or unknowingly caused by me.

I will always hold aloft an unfading torch-light of continuous kindness to guide the hearts of those who misunderstand me.

I wipe away my tears of sorrow, finding it does not matter to Thee whether I play a big or a small part, so long as I play it well.

I will seek God first; then all my desires will be satisfied. Whether I live in a palace or in a hut will make no difference.

I will use my honestly acquired money to live simply, doing away with luxury.

I make up my mind that nobody can excite me by insulting words or deeds, and that nobody can influence me by praise to think I am greater than I am.

I will care nothing for cruel, false criticism nor for garlands of praise. My sole desire is to do Thy will, to please Thee, my Heavenly Father.

I will speak the truth, but I will at all times avoid speaking unpleasant or harmful truths. I will offer no criticism that is not motivated by kindness.

I will spread the sunshine of my goodwill wherever the darkness of misunderstanding lies.

ON HUMILITY AND PRIDE

ALL MY POWERS are but borrowed powers from Thee. No one is greater than Thee, O my Father! I would cease to live and express without Thy wisdom and strength. Thou art so big; I am so little.

Train me not to be proud. Thou art the Guru-Preceptor, teaching in the temple of all souls. I bow to Thee at the feet of everyone.

I will conquer pride by humility, wrath by love, excitement by calmness, selfishness by unselfishness, evil by good, ignorance by knowledge, and restlessness by the ineffable peace acquired in the stillness of inner silence.

I will take pride in being humble. I will feel honored when chastised for doing God's work. I will rejoice for any opportunity to give love for hatred.

On Worldly Pleasures

Wisdom's fire is burning. I am feeding the flame. No use sorrowing more! All perishable pleasures, all temporary aspirations I am using as fagots to feed the eternal fire of knowledge. The old cherished logs of desire that I had saved to fashion furniture of pleasures, I cast into the hungry flames.

Ah, my myriad ambitions are crackling joyously at the touch of God's flame. My ancient home of passions, of possessions, of incarnations, of many kingdoms of my fancy, of many air castles of my dreams—all are being consumed by this fire of my own kindling.

I am beholding this blaze not with sadness but with joy, for that fire has not only burned my home of matter but all the sorrow-haunted buildings of my fancy. I am glad beyond the wealth of kings.

I am king of myself, not a fancy-enslaved king of possessions. I own nothing, yet I am the ruler of my own imperishable kingdom of peace. I am no longer a slave serving my fears of possible losses. I have nothing to lose. I am enthroned in perennial satisfaction. I am a king indeed.

Overcoming Temptation

TEACH ME, O Spirit, to distinguish between the soul's lasting happiness and the temporary pleasures of the senses.

Teach me not to engross myself in passing sense-pleasures. Teach me to discipline my senses that they may always make me really happy. Teach me to substitute for flesh temptation the greater allurement of soul happiness.

I laugh at all fears, for my Father-Mother, beloved God, is attentively awake and present everywhere with the deliberate purpose of protecting me from the temptations of evil.

O Eternal Conqueror! teach me to train noble qualities within me—soldiers of calmness and self-control. Be Thou their Divine General in the battle against the dark foes: anger, ingratitude, untruthfulness. May I raise over the realm of my life Thy flag of invincible righteousness.

O Father, train the children of my senses not to wander away from Thy home. Turn my eyes within to gaze upon Thine ever-changing beauty; train my ears to listen to Thine inward song.

Divine Mother, teach me to be so much attached to Thee that I cannot become bound to material pleasures. Teach me by Thy love to conquer all desire for a worldly life.

Divine Teacher, discipline my unwise wayward senses; spiritualize their pleasures, that they ever look beyond the illusion of glittering visible forms to find the divine joys of simplicity.

TO DEVELOP WILL

TODAY I WILL make up my mind to succeed in whatever I do. Will power is a tremendous factor in all activities. It can start endless motions of cosmic energy.

O Eternal Energy, awaken in me conscious will, conscious vitality, conscious health, conscious realization.

Teach me, O Spirit, to cooperate with Thy will until all my thoughts shall conform to Thy harmonious plans.

There is hidden strength within me to

overcome all obstacles and temptations. I will bring forth that indomitable power and energy.

Invincible Lord, teach me to use my will unceasingly in the performance of good actions, until the little light of my will burns as the cosmic blaze of Thine all-powerful will.

Beloved Father, I know that by strong will power I can overcome disease, failure, and ignorance, but the will vibration must be stronger than the vibration of physical or mental disease. The more chronic the disease, the stronger, steadier, and more unflinching must be my determination, faith, and effort of will.

Today I will cultivate initiative. The man of initiative creates something from nothing; he makes the impossible possible by the great inventive power of Spirit.

Heavenly Father, help me to strengthen my will power. Teach me not to be enslaved by habits. Guide me, that I may develop myself spiritually by inner and outer discipline.

I will tune my free will with the infinite will of God, and my only desire shall be to do the will of Him who placed me here.

WISDOM AND UNDERSTANDING

SINCE THINE INDELIBLE image of perfection is in me, teach me to wipe away the superficial stains of ignorance and to know that Thou and I are, and always have been, one.

May all demoniac noisy thoughts take flight, that Thy silent song-whispers of guidance be audible to my forgetful soul.

I will behold wisdom in ignorance, joy in sorrow, health in weakness; for I know that God's perfection is the only reality.

I am an immortal child of God, living for a little while in the caravanserai* of this body. I am here to behold the tragedies and comedies of this changeable life with an attitude of unchangeable happiness.

Since God has given me all I need, I will know Him first and then use His counsel to desire and to do only what He wills.

* A caravanserai, or inn where Oriental caravans rest on their journeys, here means a temporary stopping place on the soul's journey through incarnations.

Being endowed with free choice, I am a son of God in reality. I have been dreaming that I am a mortal man. I am now awake. The dream that my soul is imprisoned in a bodily cage has vanished. I am all that my Heavenly Father is.

Each morning I will rouse the judge of my impartial introspection and ask it to try me before the tribunal of conscience. I will direct the district attorney of discrimination to prosecute the rowdy errors that steal the peace wealth of my soul.

I will build mansions of wisdom in the unfading garden of peace, resplendent with blossoms of beautiful soul-qualities.

I will strive to make myself and all others rich with God, first and last.

God the transcendental Father, God the immanent Christ Consciousness, and God the holy creative Vibratory Force, grant me wisdom to know the truth! And through my self-effort and knowledge of the law, let me climb the precious ladder of realization, to stand at last on the shining summit of attainment, face to face with the one Spirit.

Shell after shell of my yearning for Thee will break down the ramparts of delusion. With missiles of wisdom and grim guns of determination I shall destroy the fortress of my ignorance.

Dear Father, whatever conditions confront me, I know that they represent the next step in my unfoldment. I will welcome all tests because I know that within me is the intelligence to understand and the power to overcome.

I am a prince of peace sitting on the throne of poise, directing the kingdom of activity.

Instead of being absentminded, I will use my leisure moments to think of Thee.

Divine Father, this day I will make an effort to understand the great importance of wisely using my will power at all times.

I will attune myself to Thy wisdom-guided will to direct my habit-guided will.

I will cultivate calmness of mind, knowing God is ever with me. I am Spirit!

CHRISTMAS MEDITATIONS

MEDITATION FOR CHRISTMAS EVE

LIFT YOUR EYES and concentrate within. Behold the astral star of divine wisdom and let the wise thoughts in you follow that telescopic star to behold the Christ everywhere.

In that land of everlasting Christmas, of festive, omnipresent Christ Consciousness, you will find Jesus, Krishna, the saints of all religions, the great guru-preceptors waiting to give you a divine floral reception and everlasting happiness.

Prepare for the coming of baby Christ by decorating an inner Christmas tree. Around that sacred tree lay gifts of calmness, forgiveness, nobility, service, kindness, spiritual understanding, and devotion, each one wrapped in a golden covering of goodwill and bound with a silver cord of your pure sincerity.

May the Lord, on the Christmas morn of your spiritual awakening, unwrap the gorgeous presents of your heart offerings, sealed with tears of your joy and bound with cords of your eternal fidelity to Him.

He accepts only the gifts of sacred soul qualities. His acceptance will be His greatest gift to you; for it means that, in return, the gift He will bestow on you shall be nothing less than Himself. In giving Himself He shall make your heart big enough to hold Him. Your heart shall throb with Christ in everything.

Enjoy this festivity, the birth of Christ, in your mind and soul and in every living atom.

By daily meditation you will prepare the cradle of your consciousness to hold the infinite baby Christ. Every day will become a true Christmas of divine communion.

I shall be a son of God, even as Jesus was, by receiving God fully through my sacred, meditation-expanded consciousness.

A CHRISTMAS VOW

I WILL PREPARE for the coming of the Omnipresent baby Christ by cleaning the cradle of my consciousness, now rusty with selfishness, indifference, and sense attachments; and by polishing it with deep, daily, divine meditation, introspection, and discrimination. I will remodel the cradle with the dazzling soul-qualities of brotherly love, humbleness, faith, desire for God-realization, will power, self-control, renunciation, and unselfishness, that I may fittingly celebrate the birth of the Divine Child.

MEDITATION FOR CHRISTMAS MORN

CELEBRATE THE BIRTH of Christ in the cradle of your consciousness during the Christmas season. Let His vast perception in Nature, in space, and in universal love be felt within your heart.

Break the limitations of caste, color, race, religious prejudice, and inharmony, that the cradle of your heart be big enough to hold within you the Christ-love for all creation.

On every Christmas morn of your inner perception, prepare precious packages of divine qualities and deliver them to the beloved souls who gather around the Christmas tree of inner awakening* to commemorate His birth in understanding, truth, and bliss.

Celebrating the birth of omniscient, om-

---

* I.e., the spine, with its six *chakras* or centers of light and life energy.

nipresent Christ Consciousness on the joyous Christmas festivity of your inner awakening, you will find the unbroken happiness of your dreams.

Let the omniscient Christ Consciousness* come to earth a second time and be born in you, even as it was manifested in the consciousness of Jesus.

THE TRANSFIGURING CHRIST

CHRIST HAS EVER abided in me. He has preached through my consciousness to all my rowdy and hypocritical thoughts. With the magic wand of meditative intuition He has stilled the storms in the sea of my life and of many other lives. I was mentally blind, my

---

* In Sanskrit, *Kutastha Chaitanya,* the blissful consciousness in all creation that remains ever unchanged. Awareness of Spirit as immanent in every atom of vibratory creation.

will was lame; but I was healed by the awakened Christ in me.

Christ walked on the restless waters of my mind, yet the Judas of restlessness and ignorance, deluded by the Satan of sense lures, betrayed in me the Christ calmness, the Christ joy, and crucified the Divine on the cross of forgetfulness.

Christ commanded my dead wisdom to come forth from its sackcloth of delusion, and raised my wisdom to new life.

At last my will, faith, intuition, purity, hope, meditation, right desires, good habits, self-control, sense aboveness, devotion, wisdom—all these disciples obeyed the commandments of the Christ who appeared on the high mountain of my meditation.

O living Christ, present in the body of Jesus and in all of us, manifest Thyself in the essence of Thy glory, in the strength of Thy light, in the power of Thy perfect wisdom.

CHRISTMAS MEDITATION

ALL MY THOUGHTS are decorating the Christmas tree of meditation with the rare gifts of devotion, sealed with golden heart-prayers that Christ may come and receive my humble gifts.

I will mentally join in the worship in all mosques, churches, and temples; and perceive the birth of the universal Christ Consciousness as peace on the altar of all devotional hearts.

O Christ, may the birth of Thy love be felt in all hearts this Christmas and on all other days.

O Christ, bless Thy children that they inwardly cooperate with Thy laws. Make us realize that Thou art the best shelter from harm.

Teach us, O Christ, to be devoted to our Father as Thou art.

After waiting for me through many incarnations, Christ is being born anew in me. All the boundaries of my little mind are broken that the Christ-child may wake on the lap of my consciousness.

Christ Consciousness in me is the shepherd to lead my restless thoughts to my home of divine peace.

O Lord! make my heart big enough to hold Thee, that it throb with the Christ

Consciousness in everything. Then shall I enjoy the festivity of Thy birth in my mind, my soul, and in oneness with every pulsing atom.

ABOUT THE AUTHOR

Paramahansa Yogananda (1893–1952) is widely regarded as one of the preeminent spiritual figures of our time. Born in northern India, he came to the United States in 1920, where for more than thirty years he taught India's ancient science of meditation and the art of balanced spiritual living. Through his acclaimed life story, *Autobiography of a Yogi,* and his numerous other books, he has introduced millions of readers to the timeless truths underlying the religious traditions of East and West.

In 1920, Paramahansa Yogananda founded Self-Realization Fellowship (known in India as Yogoda Satsanga Society of India) to make available the teachings he had brought to the West. Among the aims and ideals he envisioned for his society are: disseminating scientific techniques for attaining direct personal experience of God, showing the basic principles of truth that are the common foundation of all true religions, and thereby promoting a spirit of greater harmony among the diverse people and nations of the world.

Through his practical "how-to-live" teachings, Paramahansa Yogananda sought to give people of all races and creeds the means to free themselves from physical, mental, and spiritual inharmonies, and to realize and express more fully in their lives the beauty, nobility, and true divinity of the human spirit. His worldwide work continues today under the guidance of one of his earliest and closest disciples, Sri Daya Mata, president of Self-Realization Fellowship.

PARAMAHANSA YOGANANDA:
A YOGI IN LIFE AND DEATH

Paramahansa Yogananda entered *mahasamadhi* (a yogi's final conscious exit from the body) in Los Angeles, California, on March 7, 1952, after concluding his speech at a banquet held in honor of H.E. Binay R. Sen, Ambassador of India.

The great world teacher demonstrated the value of yoga (scientific techniques for God-realization) not only in life but in death. Weeks after his departure his unchanged face shone with the divine luster of incorruptibility.

Mr. Harry T. Rowe, Los Angeles Mortuary Director, Forest Lawn Memorial-Park (in which the body of the great master is temporarily placed), sent Self-Realization Fellowship a notarized letter from which the following extracts are taken:

"The absence of any visual signs of decay in the dead body of Paramahansa Yogananda offers the most extraordinary case in our experience....No physical disintegration was visible in his body even twenty days after death....No indication of mold was visible on his skin, and no visible desiccation (drying up) took place in the bodily tissues. This state of perfect preservation of a body is, so far as we know from mortuary annals, an unparalleled one....At the time of receiving Yogananda's body, the Mortuary personnel expected to observe, through the glass lid of the casket, the usual progressive signs of bodily decay. Our astonishment increased as day followed day without bringing any visible change in the body under observation. Yogananda's body was apparently in a phenomenal state of immutability....

"No odor of decay emanated from his body at any time....The physical appearance of Yogananda on March 27th, just before the bronze cover of the casket was put into position, was the same as it had been on March 7th. He looked on March 27th as fresh and as unravaged by decay as he had looked on the night of his death. On March 27th there was no reason to say that his body had suffered any visible physical disintegration at all. For these reasons we state again that the case of Paramahansa Yogananda is unique in our experience."

ALSO BY
PARAMAHANSA YOGANANDA

Available at bookstores or directly from the publisher

Autobiography of a Yogi

In the Sanctuary of the Soul: *A Guide To Effective Prayer*

Where There Is Light: *Insight and Inspiration for
Meeting Life's Challenges*

How You Can Talk With God

The Law of Success

Scientific Healing Affirmations

The Science of Religion

Man's Eternal Quest

The Divine Romance

Journey to Self-realization: *Discovering the
Gifts of the Soul*

God Talks With Arjuna: *The Bhagavad Gita—
A New Translation and Commentary*

Wine of the Mystic: *The Rubaiyat of
Omar Khayyam—A Spiritual Interpretation*

Whispers from Eternity

Sayings of Paramahansa Yogananda

Songs of the Soul

Cosmic Chants

Self-Realization Fellowship
3880 San Rafael Avenue • Los Angeles, California 90065-3298
Tel (323) 225-2471 • Fax (323) 225-5088
www.yogananda-srf.org